ON THE USE OF PHILOSOPHY

Three Essays

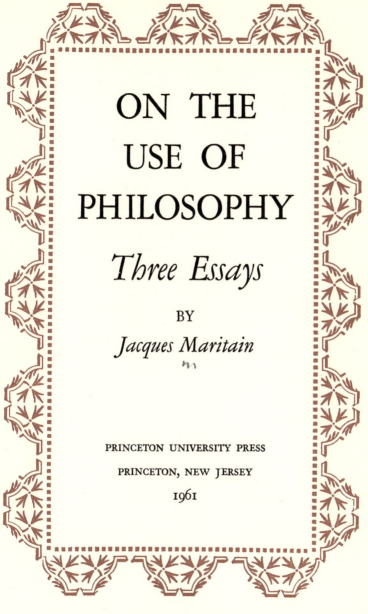

ON THE
USE OF
PHILOSOPHY

Three Essays

BY

Jacques Maritain

PRINCETON UNIVERSITY PRESS

PRINCETON, NEW JERSEY

1961

The first and second essays in this book,
"The Philosopher in Society" and "Truth
and Human Fellowship," were originally
given as lectures at the Graduate School
of Princeton University. "The Philosopher
in Society" also appears in *Le Philosophe
dans La Cité*, published by Alsatia, Paris,
in 1960. "Truth and Human Fellowship"
contains some extracts from *Ransoming the
Time*; copyright 1941 Charles Scribner's
Sons.

Printed in the United States of America by
Princeton University Press, Princeton, New Jersey

To

Sir Hugh Taylor

who is in many ways

responsible for this book

Homage of gratitude

and affection

CONTENTS

The Philosopher in Society   3

Truth and Human Fellowship   16

God and Science   44

ON THE USE OF PHILOSOPHY

Three Essays

THE PHILOSOPHER
IN SOCIETY

●●

The Power of the Philosopher

A PHILOSOPHER is a man in search of wisdom. Wisdom does not indeed seem to be an exceedingly widespread commodity; there has never been overproduction in this field. The greater the scarcity of what the philosopher is supposed to be concerned with, the more we feel inclined to think that society needs the philosopher badly.

Unfortunately there is no such thing as *the* philosopher; this dignified abstraction exists only in our minds. There are philosophers; and philosophers, as soon as they philosophize, are, or seem to be, in disagreement on everything, even on the first principles of philosophy. Each one goes his own way. They question every matter of common assent, and their answers are conflicting. What can be expected from them for the good of society?

Moreover the greatness of a philosopher and the truth of his philosophy are independent values. Great philosophers may happen to be in the wrong. Historians bestow the honor of having been the "fathers of the modern world" upon two men, the first of whom was a great dreamer and a poor philosopher, namely Jean-Jacques Rousseau; the second a poor dreamer and a great philosopher, namely Hegel. And Hegel has involved the modern world in still more far-reaching and still more deadly errors than Rousseau did.

At least this very fact makes manifest to us the power and importance of philosophers, for good and for evil. (Aesop, if I remember correctly, said as much of that valuable organ—the tongue.) If bad philosophy is a plague for society, what a blessing good philosophy must be for it! Let us not forget, moreover, that if Hegel was the father of the world of today insofar as it denies the superiority of the human person and the transcendence of God, and kneels before history, St. Augustine was the father of Christian Western civilization, in which the world of today, despite all threats and failures, still participates.

To look at things in a more analytical way, let us say that in actual existence society cannot do without philosophers.

Even when they are in the wrong, philosophers are a kind of mirror, on the heights of intelligence, of the deepest trends which are obscurely at play in the human mind at each epoch of history; (the greater they are, the more actively and powerfully radiant the mirror is). Now, since we are thinking beings, such mirrors are indispensable to us. After all, it is better for human society to have Hegelian errors with Hegel than to have Hegelian errors without Hegel—I mean hidden and diffuse errors rampant throughout the social body, which are Hegelian in type but anonymous and unrecognizable. A great philosopher in the wrong is like a beacon on the reefs, which says to seamen: steer clear of me. He enables men (at least those who have not been seduced by him) to *identify* the errors from which they suffer, and to become clearly aware of them, and to struggle against them. This is an essential need of society, insofar as society is not merely animal society, but society made up of persons endowed with intelligence and freedom.

Even if philosophers are hopelessly divided among themselves in their search for a superior and all-pervading truth, at least they seek this truth; and their very controversies, constantly renewed, are a sign of the necessity for such a search. These controversies do not witness to the illusory or unattainable character of the object that philosophers are looking for. They witness to the fact that this object is so difficult because it is crucial in importance: is not everything which is crucial in importance crucial also in difficulty? Plato told us that beautiful things are difficult, and that we should not avoid beautiful dangers. Mankind would be in jeopardy, and soon in despair, if it shunned the beautiful dangers of intelligence and reason. Moreover many things are questionable and oversimplified in the commonplace insistence on the insuperable disagreements which divide philosophers. These disagreements do indeed exist. But in one sense there is more continuity and stability in philosophy than in science. For a new scientific theory completely changes the very manner in which the former ones posed the question, whereas philosophical problems remain always the same, in one form or another. Nay more, basic philosophical ideas, once they have been discovered, become permanent acquisitions in the philosophical heritage. They are used in various, even opposite ways: they are still there. Finally, philosophers quarrel so violently because each one has seen some truth which, more often than not, has dazzled his eyes, and which he may conceptualize in an insane manner, but of which his fellow-philosophers must also be aware, each in his own perspective.

What Is the Use of Philosophy?

At this point we come to the essential consideration: what is the use of philosophy? Philosophy, taken in itself, is above utility. And for this very reason philosophy is of the utmost necessity for men. It reminds them of the supreme utility of those things which do not deal with means, but with ends. For men do not live only by bread, vitamins, and technological discoveries. They live by values and realities which are above time, and are worth being known for their own sake; they feed on that invisible food which sustains the life of the spirit, and which makes them aware, not of such or such means at the service of their life, but of their very reasons for living—and suffering, and hoping.

The philosopher in society witnesses to the supreme dignity of thought; he points to what is eternal in man, and stimulates our thirst for pure knowledge and disinterested knowledge, for knowledge of those fundamentals—about the nature of things and the nature of the mind, and man himself, and God—which are superior to, and independent of, anything we can make or produce or create—and to which all our practice is appendent, because we think before acting and nothing can limit the range of thought: our practical decisions depend on the stand we take on the ultimate questions that human thought is able to ask. That is why philosophical systems, which are directed toward no practical use and application, have, as I remarked at the beginning, such an impact on human history.

The advocates of dialectical materialism claim that philosophy does not have to contemplate, but to transform the world: because philosophy is essentially *praxis*, instrument for action, power exercised on things. This is but a return to the old magical confusion between knowledge and power, a perfect disregard of the function of thought. Philosophy is essentially a disinterested activity, directed toward truth loved for its own sake, not utilitarian activity for the sake of power over things. That is why we need it. If philosophy is one of the forces which contribute to the movement of history and the changes that occur in the world, it is because philosophy, in its primary task, which is the metaphysical penetration of being, is intent only on discerning and contemplating what is the truth of certain matters which have importance in themselves and for themselves, independently of what happens in the world, and which, precisely for that reason, exert an essential influence on the world.

Two aspects of the function of the philosopher in society have, it seems to me, special significance today. They have to do with Truth and Freedom.

The great danger which threatens modern societies is a weakening of the sense of Truth. On the one hand men become so accustomed to thinking in terms of stimuli and responses, and adjustment to environment; on the other hand they are so bewildered by the manner in which the political techniques of advertising and propaganda use the words of the language that they are tempted finally to give up any interest in truth: only practical results, or sheer material verification of facts and figures, matter for them, without internal adherence to any truth really grasped. The philosopher who in pursuing his speculative task pays no attention to the interests of men, or of the social group, or of the state, reminds society of the absolute and unbending character of Truth.

As to Freedom, he reminds society that freedom is the very condition for the exercise of thought. This is a requirement of the common good itself of human society, which disintegrates as soon as fear, superseding inner conviction, imposes any kind of shibboleth upon human minds. The philosopher, even when he is wrong, at least freely criticizes many things his fellowmen are attracted to. Socrates bore witness to this function of criticism which is inherent in philosophy. Even though society showed its gratitude to him in quite a peculiar way, he remains the great example of the philosopher in society. It is not without reason that Napoleon loathed *idéologues*, and that dictators, as a rule, hate philosophers.

Moral Philosophy

I have spoken above all of speculative or theoretical philosophy, the chief part of which is metaphysics. The name of Socrates calls forth another kind of philosophy, namely moral or practical philosophy.

Here the need of society for philosophy, and for sound philosophy, appears in a more immediate and urgent manner.

It has been often observed that science provides us

with means—more and more powerful, more and more wondrous means. These means can be used either for good or for evil, depending on the ends to which they are used. The determination of the true and genuine ends of human life is not within the province of science. It is within the province of wisdom. In other words, it is within the province of philosophy—and, to tell the truth, not of philosophical wisdom alone, but also of God-given wisdom. Society needs philosophers in this connection. It needs saints even more.

On the other hand the human sciences—psychology, sociology, anthropology—afford us with invaluable and ever-growing material dealing with the behavior of individual and collective man and with the basic components of human life and civilization. This is an immense help in our effort to penetrate the world of man. But all this material and this immense treasure of facts would be of no avail if it were not interpreted, so as to enlighten us on *what man is*. It is up to the philosopher to undertake this task of interpretation.

My point is that society is in special need of this sort of work. For merely material *information*, or any kind of Kinsey report, on human mores, is rather of a nature to shatter the root beliefs of any given society, as long as it is not accompanied by genuine knowledge of man, which depends, in the last analysis, on wisdom and philosophy. Only the philosophical knowledge of man permits us, for example, to distinguish between what is conformable to the nature and reason of man, and the way in which men do in fact conduct themselves, indeed in the majority of cases; in other words, to distinguish between the modes of behavior which are really *normal* and the modes of comportment which are statistically frequent.

Finally when it comes to moral values and moral standards, the consideration of our present world authorizes us to make the following remark: it is a great misfortune that a civilization should suffer from a cleavage between the ideal which constitutes its reason for living and acting, and for which it continues to fight, and the inner cast of mind which exists in people, and which implies in reality doubt and mental insecurity about this same ideal. As a matter of fact, the common psyche of a society or a civilization, the memory of past experiences, family and community traditions, and the sort of emotional temperament, or vegetative structure of feeling, which have been thus engendered, may maintain in the practical conduct of men a deep-seated devotion to standards and values in which their intellect has ceased to believe. Under such circumstances they are even prepared to die, if necessary, for refusing to commit some unethical action or for defending justice or freedom, but they are at a loss to find any rational justification for the notions of justice, freedom, ethical behavior; these things no longer have for their minds any objective and unconditional value, perhaps any meaning. Such a situation is possible; it cannot last. A time will come when people will give up in practical existence those values about which they no longer have any intellectual conviction. Hence we realize how necessary the function of a sound moral philosophy is in human society. It has to give, or to give back, to society intellectual faith in the value of its ideals.

These remarks apply to democratic society in a particularly cogent way, for the foundations of a society of free men are essentially moral. There are a certain number of moral tenets—about the dignity of the human person, human rights, human equality, freedom, law, mutual respect and tolerance, the unity of mankind and the ideal of peace among men—on which democracy presupposes common consent; without a general, firm, and reasoned-out conviction concerning such tenets, democracy cannot survive. It is not the job of scientists, experts, specialists, and technicians, it is the job of philosophers to look for the rational justification and elucidation of the democratic charter. In this sense it is not uncalled-for to say that the philosopher plays in society as to principles, as im-

portant a part as the statesman as to practical govern-
ment. Both may be great destroyers if they are mistaken. Both may be genuine servants of the common
good, if they are on the right road. Nothing is more
immediately necessary for our times than a sound
political philosophy.

I would betray my own convictions if I did not
add that—given on the one hand the state of confusion and division in which the modern mind finds
itself, on the other hand the fact that the deepest incentive of democratic thought is, as Henri Bergson
observed, a repercussion of the Gospel's inspiration in
the temporal order—philosophy, especially moral and
political philosophy, can perform its normal function
in our modern society, especially as regards the need
of democratic society for a genuine rational establish-
ment of its common basic tenets, only if it keeps vital
continuity with the spirit of the Judaeo-Christian
tradition and with the wisdom of the Gospel, in other
words, if it is a work and effort of human reason intent on the most exacting requirements of philosophical method and principles, equipped with all the
weapons and information of contemporary science,
and guided by the light of the supreme truths of
which Christian faith makes us aware.

I know that the notion of Christian philosophy is a
controversial notion, and rather complicated. I have

no intention of discussing the problem here. I should like only to point out that we cannot help posing it. As for myself, the more I think of the relationship between philosophy and theology in the course of history, the more I am convinced that in concrete existence this problem is solved in a way favorable to the notion of Christian philosophy.

One final point should be touched upon; I will limit myself to a few remarks on it. It has to do with the philosopher's attitude toward human, social, political affairs.

Needless to say, a philosopher may set aside his philosophical pursuits and become a man of politics. But what of a philosopher who remains simply a philosopher, and acts only as a philosopher?

On the one hand we may suppose, without fear of being wrong, that he lacks the experience, the information, and the competence which are proper to a man of action: it would be a misfortune for him to undertake to legislate in social and political matters in the name of pure logic, as Plato did.

But, on the other hand, the philosopher cannot—especially in our time—shut himself up in an ivory tower; he cannot help being concerned about human affairs, in the name of philosophy itself and by reason of the very values which philosophy has to defend and maintain. He has to *bear witness* to these values, every time they are attacked, as in the time of Hitler when insane racist theories worked to provoke the mass murder of Jews, or as today before the threat of enslavement by communist despotism. The philosopher must bear witness by expressing his thoughts and telling the truth as he sees it. This may have repercussions in the domain of politics; it is not, in itself, a political action—it is simply applied philosophy.

It is true that the line of demarcation is difficult to draw. This means that no one, not even philosophers, can avoid taking risks, when justice or love are at stake, and when one is face to face with the strict command of the Gospel: *haec oportuit facere, et illa non omittere*, "these ought ye to have done, and not to leave the other undone."[1]

[1] Matthew 23:23.

TRUTH AND HUMAN
FELLOWSHIP

....

*Si fieri potest, quod ex vobis est, cum
omnibus hominibus pacem habentes.*
St. Paul, Rom. 12:18.

If it be possible, as much as lieth in
you, live peaceably with all men.

....

Absolutism and Relativism

"O LIBERTY, how many crimes are committed in thy name!" Madame Roland said, mounting the scaffold. O Truth, it may be said, how often blind violence and oppression have been let loose in thy name in the course of history! "Zeal for truth," as Father Victor White puts it, "has too often been a cloak for the most evil and revolting of human passions."[1]

As a result, some people think that in order to set human existence free from these evil passions, and make men live in peace and pleasant quiet, the best way is to get rid of any zeal for truth or attachment to truth.

[1] Rev. Father Victor White, O.P., "Religious Tolerance," *The Commonweal*, September 4, 1953.

[16]

Thus it is that after the violence and cruelty of wars of religion, a period of skepticism usually occurs, as at the time of Montaigne and Charron.

Here we have only the swing of the pendulum moving from one extreme to another. Skepticism, moreover, may happen to hold those who are not skeptical to be barbarous, childish, or subhuman, and it may happen to treat them as badly as the zealot treats the unbeliever. Then skepticism proves to be as intolerant as fanaticism—it becomes the fanaticism of doubt. This is a sign that skepticism is not the answer.

The answer is humility, together with faith in truth.

The problem of truth and human fellowship is important for democratic societies; it seems to me to be particularly important for this country, where men and women coming from a great diversity of national stocks and religious or philosophical creeds have to live together. If each one of them endeavored to impose his own convictions and the truth in which he believes on all his co-citizens, would not living together become impossible? That is obviously right. Well, it is easy, too easy, to go a step further, and to ask: if each one sticks to his own convictions, will not each one endeavor to impose his own convictions on all others? So that, as a result, living together will become impossible if any citizen whatever sticks to his own convictions and believes in a given truth?

Thus it is not unusual to meet people who think that *not to believe in any truth*, or *not to adhere firmly to any assertion as unshakeably true in itself*, is a primary condition required of democratic citizens in order to be tolerant of one another and to live in peace with one another. May I say that these people are in fact the most intolerant people, for if perchance they were to believe in something as unshakeably true, they would feel compelled, by the same stroke, to impose by force and coercion their own belief on their co-citizens. The only remedy they have found to get rid of their abiding tendency to fanaticism is to cut themselves off from truth. That is a suicidal method. It is a suicidal conception of democracy: not only would a democratic society which lived on universal skepticism condemn itself to death by starvation; but it would also enter a process of self-annihilation, from the very fact that no democratic society can live without a common practical belief in those truths which are freedom, justice, law, and the other tenets of democracy; and that any belief in these things as objectively and unshakeably true, as well as in any other kind of truth, would be brought to naught by the preassumed law of universal skepticism.

In the field of political science, the opinion which I am criticizing was made into a theory—the so-called "relativistic justification of democracy"—by Hans

Kelsen. It is very significant that in order to establish his philosophy of the temporal order and show that democracy implies ignorance of, or doubt about, any absolute truth, either religious or metaphysical, Kelsen has recourse to Pilate; so that, in refusing to distinguish the just from the unjust, and washing his hands, this dishonest judge thus becomes the lofty precursor of relativistic democracy. Kelsen quotes the dialogue between Jesus and Pilate—John, Chapter 18 —in which Jesus says: "To this end am I come into the world, that I should bear witness unto the truth," and Pilate answers: "What is truth?" and then delivers Jesus over to the fury of the crowd. Because Pilate did not know what truth is, Kelsen concludes, he therefore called upon the people, and asked them to decide; and thus in a democratic society it is up to the people to decide, and mutual tolerance reigns, because no one knows what truth is.

The truth of which Kelsen was speaking was religious and metaphysical truth—what they call "absolute truth," as if any truth, insofar as it is true, were not absolute in its own sphere. As Miss Helen Silving puts it,[2] the burden of Kelsen's argument is: "Whoever knows or claims to know absolute truth or absolute justice"—that is to say, *truth* or *justice* simply —"cannot be a democrat, because he cannot and is

[2] Helen Silving, "The Conflict of Liberty and Equality," *Iowa Law Review*, Spring 1950.

not expected to admit the possibility of a view different from his own, the *true* view. The metaphysician and the believer are bound to impose their eternal truth on other people, on the ignorant, and on the people without vision. Theirs is the holy crusade of the one who knows against the one who does not know or does not share in God's grace. Only if we are aware of our ignorance of what is the *Good* may we call upon the people to decide."

It is impossible to summarize more accurately a set of more barbarous and erroneous assumptions. If it were true that whoever knows or claims to know truth or justice cannot admit the possibility of a view different from his own, and is bound to impose his true view on other people by violence, then the rational animal would be the most dangerous of beasts. In reality it is through rational means, that is, through persuasion, not through coercion, that the rational animal is bound by his very nature to try to induce his fellow men to share in what he knows or claims to know as true or just. The metaphysician, because he trusts human reason, and the believer, because he trusts divine grace and knows that "a forced faith is a hypocrisy hateful to God and man," as Cardinal Manning put it, do not use holy war to make their "eternal truth" accessible to other people; they appeal to the inner freedom of other people by offering them either their demonstrations or the testimony of their love. And we do not call upon the people to decide because we are aware of our ignorance of what is the good, but because we know this truth and this good, that the people have a right to self-government.

It is, no doubt, easy to observe that in the history of mankind nothing goes to show that, from primitive times on, religious feeling or religious ideas have been particularly successful in pacifying men; religious differences seem rather to have fed and sharpened their conflicts. On the one hand truth always makes trouble, and those who bear witness to it are always persecuted: "Do not think that I came to send peace upon earth; I came not to send peace, but the sword."[3] On the other hand—and this is the point we must face—those who know or claim to know truth happen sometimes to persecute others. I do not deny the fact; I say that this fact, like all other facts, needs to be understood. It only means that, given the weakness of our nature, the impact of the highest and most sacred things upon the coarseness of the human heart is liable to make these things, by accident, a prey to its passions, as long as it has not been purified by genuine love. It is nonsense to regard fanaticism as a fruit of religion. Fanaticism is a natural tendency rooted in our basic egotism and will to power. It seizes upon any noble feeling to live on it. The only remedy for religious fanaticism is the Gospel light and the

[3] Matthew 10:34.

progress of religious consciousness in faith itself and in that fraternal love which is the fruit of the human soul's union with God. For then man realizes the sacred transcendence of truth and of God. The more he grasps truth, through science, philosophy, or faith, the more he feels what immensity remains to be grasped within this very truth. The more he knows God, either by reason or by faith, the more he understands that our concepts attain (through analogy) but do not circumscribe Him, and that His thoughts are not like our thoughts: for "who hath known the mind of the Lord, or who hath become His counselor?"[4] The more strong and deep faith becomes, the more man kneels down, not before his own alleged ignorance of truth, but before the inscrutable mystery of divine truth, and before the hidden ways in which God goes to meet those who search Him.

To sum up, the real problem has to do with the human subject, endowed as he is with his rights in relation to his fellow men, and afflicted as he is by the vicious inclinations which derive from his will to power. On the one hand, the error of the absolutists who would like to impose truth by coercion comes from the fact that they shift their right feelings about the object from the object to the subject; and they think that just as error has no rights of its own and

[4] Isaias 40:13.

should be banished from the mind (through the means of the mind), so man when he is in error has no rights of his own and should be banished from human fellowship (through the means of human power).

On the other hand, the error of the theorists who make relativism, ignorance, and doubt a necessary condition for mutual tolerance comes from the fact that they shift their right feelings about the human subject—who must be respected even if he is in error —from the subject to the object; and thus they deprive man and the human intellect of the very act— adherence to the truth—in which consists both man's dignity and reason for living.

They begin, as we have seen apropos of Kelsen, with the supreme truths either of metaphysics or of faith. But science also deals with truth, though in science the discovery of a new truth supplants most often a previous theory which was hitherto considered true. What will happen if human fanaticism takes hold of what it claims to be scientific truth at a given moment? Suffice it to look at the manner in which the Stalinist state imposed on scientists its own physical, biological, linguistic, or economic truth. Shall we then conclude that in order to escape state-science oppression or management, the only way is to give up science and scientific truth, and to take refuge in ignorance?

It is truth, not ignorance, which makes us humble, and gives us the sense of what remains unknown in our very knowledge. In one sense only is there wisdom in appealing to our ignorance: if we mean the ignorance of those who know, not the ignorance of those who are in the dark.

Be it a question of science, metaphysics, or religion, the man who says: "What is truth?" as Pilate did, is not a tolerant man, but a betrayer of the human race. There is real and genuine tolerance only when a man is firmly and absolutely convinced of a truth, or of what he holds to be a truth, and when he at the same time recognizes the right of those who deny this truth to exist, and to contradict him, and to speak their own mind, not because they are free from truth but because they seek truth in their own way, and because he respects in them human nature and human dignity and those very resources and living springs of the intellect and of conscience which make them potentially capable of attaining the truth he loves, if someday they happen to see it.

Can Philosophers Cooperate?

A particular application of the problem we are discussing can be found in the philosophical field. Some years ago I was asked whether in my opinion philosophers can cooperate.

I felt rather embarrassed by this question, for on

the one hand if philosophy is not search for truth it is nothing, and truth admits of no compromise; on the other hand if philosophers, that is, lovers of wisdom, cannot cooperate, how will any human cooperation be possible? The fact that philosophical discussions seem to consist of deaf men's quarrels is not reassuring for civilization.

My answer is that philosophers do not cooperate, as a rule, because human nature is as weak in them as in any other poor devil of a rational animal, but that they *can* cooperate; and that cooperation between philosophers can only be a conquest of the intellect over itself and the very universe of thought it has created—a difficult conquest indeed, achieved by intellectual rigor and justice on the basis of irreducible and inevitably lasting antagonisms.

A distinction, moreover, seems to me to be relevant in this connection. The question can be considered either from the point of view of *doctrinal exchanges* between systems or from the point of view of the *mutual grasp* which various philosophical systems can have of each other, each being taken as a whole.

From the first point of view, or the point of view of doctrinal exchanges, each system can avail itself of the others for its own sake by dismembering them, and by feeding on and assimilating what it can take from them. That is cooperation indeed, but in quite a peculiar sense—as a lion cooperates with a lamb.

Yet from the second point of view, and in the perspective of the judgment which each system passes on the other, contemplating it as a whole, and as an object situated in an external sphere, and trying to do it justice, a mutual understanding is possible which cannot indeed do away with basic antagonisms, but which may create a kind of real though imperfect cooperation, to the extent that each system succeeds (1) in recognizing for the other, in a certain sense, a right to exist; and (2) in availing itself of the other, no longer by material *intussusception* and by borrowing or digesting parts of the other, but by bringing, thanks to the other, its own specific life and principles to a higher degree of achievement and extension.

It is on this genuine kind of cooperation that I would like to insist for a moment.

If we were able to realize that most often our mutually opposed affirmations do not bear on the same parts or aspects of the real and that they are of greater value than our mutual negations, then we should come nearer the first prerequisite of a genuinely philosophical understanding: that is, we should become better able to transcend and conquer our own system of signs and conceptual language, and to take on for a moment, in a provisional and tentative manner, the thought and approach of the other so as to come back, with this intelligible booty, to our own

philosophical conceptualization and to our own system of reference.

Then, we are no longer concerned with analyzing
or *sorting* the set of assertions peculiar to various systems in spreading them out, so to speak, on a single
surface or level in order to examine what conciliation
or exchange of ideas they may mutually allow in their
inner structure. But we are concerned with taking
into account a third dimension, in order to examine
the manner in which each system, considered as a
specific whole, can, according to its own frame of
reference, do justice to the other in taking a view of it
and seeking to penetrate it as an object situated on
the outside—in another sphere of thought.

From this standpoint, two considerations would
appear all-important: the one is the consideration of
the central *intuition* which lies at the core of each
great philosophical doctrine; the other is the consideration of the *place* which each system could, according to its own frame of reference, grant the other
system as the legitimate place the latter is cut out to
occupy in the universe of thought.

Actually, each great philosophical doctrine lives
on a central intuition which can be wrongly concep-
tualized and translated into a system of assertions
seriously deficient or erroneous as such, but which,
insofar as it is intellectual intuition, truly gets hold
of some aspect of the real. Consequently, each great

philosophical doctrine, once it has been grasped in its central intuition and then re-interpreted in the frame of reference of another doctrine (in a manner that it would surely not accept), should be granted from the point of view of this other doctrine some place considered as legitimately occupied, be it in some imaginary universe.

If we try to do justice to the philosophical systems against which we take our most determined stand, we shall seek to discover both that intuition which they involve and that place we must grant them from our own point of view. Then we shall benefit from them, not by borrowing from them or exchanging with them certain particular views and ideas, but by seeing, thanks to them, more profoundly into our own doctrine, by enriching it from within and extending its principles to new fields of inquiry which have been brought more forcefully to our attention, but which we shall make all the more vitally and powerfully informed by these principles.

Thus there is not *toleration* between systems—a system cannot *tolerate* another system, because systems are abstract sets of ideas and have only intellectual existence, where the will to tolerate or not to tolerate has no part—but there can be *justice*, intellectual justice, between philosophical systems.

Between philosophers there can be tolerance and more than tolerance; there can be a kind of cooperation and fellowship, founded on intellectual justice and the philosophical duty of understanding another's thought in a genuine and fair manner. Nay more, there is no intellectual justice without the assistance of intellectual charity. If we do not *love* the thought and intellect of another as intellect and thought, how shall we take pains to discover what truths are conveyed by it while it seems to us defective or misguided, and at the same time to free these truths from the errors which prey upon them and to re-instate them in an entirely true systematization? Thus we love truth more than we do our fellow-philosophers, but we love and respect both.

Mutual Understanding between Men of Different Religious Faiths

At this point it would be relevant to return to certain observations I made in the preceding chapter.[5] At least I would like to insist on the remark that the constantly renewed controversies between philosophers bear witness to the necessity of the search for a superior and all-pervading truth.

The more deeply we look into these controversies, the more we realize that they thrive on a certain number (increasing with the progress of time) of basic themes to which each newly arriving philosopher endeavors to give some kind of place—however uncom-

[5] See *supra,* pp. 4-7.

fortable, and though acquired at the price of con-
sistency—in his own system, while at the same time,
more often than not, his overemphasis on one of the
themes in question causes his system to be at odds
with those of his fellow-competitors—and with the
truth of the matter.

The greater and truer a philosophy, the more perfect the balance between all the ever-recurrent basic
themes with whose discordant claims philosophical
reflection has to do.

At first glance it seems particularly shocking, as I
previously observed, that men dedicated to wisdom and to the grasping of the highest truths might
be not only in mutual disagreement—which is quite
normal—but might display, as actually happens with
saddening frequency, more mutual intolerance—refusing one another any right intellectually to exist—
than even potters, as Aristotle put it, or painters and
writers with respect to each other. In reality this is not
surprising, for mutual toleration relates essentially to
living together in concrete existence; and, as a result,
mutual toleration is easier in practical matters than
in theoretical ones. When it is a question of rescuing
a man from a fire, mutual toleration and cooperation
between an atheist and a Christian, or an advocate of
determinism and an advocate of free will, will be a
matter of course. But when it comes to knowing the
truth about the nature of the human will, the cooperation between the advocate of determinism and

the advocate of free will will become more difficult. We just saw on what conditions and in overcoming what obstacles such cooperation between philosophers is possible. To tell the truth, philosophers are naturally intolerant, and genuine tolerance among them means a great victory of virtue over nature in their minds. The same can be said, I am afraid, of theologians. This theme was particularly dear to Descartes, who made theologians (non-Cartesian theologians) responsible for all wars in the world. Yet both philosophers and theologians are surely able to overcome the natural bent I just alluded to, and to nurture all the more respect for the man in error as they are more eager to vindicate the truth he disregards or disfigures.

Thus we come to our third point: mutual understanding and cooperation—in uncompromising fidelity to truth as each one sees it—between men of different faiths: I do not mean on the temporal level and for temporal tasks; I mean on the very level of religious life, knowledge, and experience.[6] If it is true that human society must bring together, in the service of the same terrestrial common good, men belonging to different spiritual families, how can the peace of that temporal society be lastingly assured if first in the domain that matters most to the human being—

[6] See "Who Is My Neighbor?" in *Ransoming the Time* (New York: Charles Scribner's Sons, 1941), pp. 116, 117, 123, 124.

in the spiritual and religious domain itself—relation-ships of mutual respect and mutual understanding cannot be established?

I prefer the word "fellowship" to "tolerance" for a number of reasons. In the first place, the word *tolerance* relates not only to the virtue of mutual tol-eration between human individuals, which I am dis-cussing here, but also to problems which are ex-traneous to my present topic. For instance, on the one hand there is the problem of "dogmatic toler-ance": has man a moral obligation to seek religious truth and to cling to it when he sees it? Yes indeed. Has the Church a right to condemn errors opposed to the deposit of divine revelation with which she has been entrusted? Yes indeed. And, on the other hand, there is the problem of "civil tolerance"[7]: Must civil society respect the realm of consciences and refrain from imposing a religious creed by coercion? Again, yes indeed.

In the second place the word *fellowship* connotes something positive—positive and elementary—in hu-man relationships. It conjures up the image of travel-ling companions, who meet here below by chance and journey through life—however fundamental their differences may be—good humoredly, in cordial

[7] See Charles Journet, *The Church of the Word Incarnate* (London and New York: Sheed and Ward, 1955), i, pp. 215-216, 283-284.

solidarity and human agreement, or better to say, friendly and cooperative disagreement. Well then, for the reasons I have just mentioned, the problem of good fellowship between the members of the various religious families seems to me to be a cardinal one for our age of civilization.

Let me say immediately that this attempt at rapprochement might easily be misunderstood. I shall therefore begin by clearing the ground of any possible sources of misunderstanding. Such a rapprochement obviously cannot be effectuated at the cost of straining fidelity, or of any yielding in intellectual integrity, or of any lessening of what is due to truth. Nor is there any question whatever either of agreeing upon I know not what common minimum of truth or of subjecting each one's convictions to a common index of doubt. On the contrary, such a coming together is only conceivable if we assume that each gives the maximum of fidelity to the light that is shown to him. Furthermore, it obviously can only be pure, and therefore valid and efficacious, if it is free from any *arrière-pensée* of a temporal nature and from even the shadow of a tendency to subordinate religion to the defense of any earthly interest or acquired advantage.

I am sure that everyone is agreed on these negative conditions I have just enumerated. But as soon as we pass on to positive considerations each one sees the very justification and the very reason for being of this good fellowship between believers of different religious families mirrored in his own particular outlook and in his own world of thought. And these outlooks are irreducibly heterogeneous; these worlds of thought never exactly meet. Until the day of eternity comes, their dimensions can have no common measure. There is no use closing one's eyes to this fact, which simply bears witness to the internal coherence of the systems of signs, built up in accordance with different principles, on which human minds depend for their cognitive life. Fundamental notions such as that of the absolute oneness of God have not the same meaning for a Jew as for a Christian; nor has the notion of the divine transcendence and incommunicability the same meaning for a Christian as for a Moslem; nor the notions of person, of freedom, grace, revelation, incarnation, of nature and the supernatural, the same meaning for the Orient as for the Occident. And the "non-violence" of the Indian is not the same as Christian "charity." No doubt, as I just said apropos of philosophical justice, it is the privilege of the human intelligence to understand other languages than the one it itself uses. It is none the less true that if, instead of being men, we were patterns of Pure Ideas, our nature would be to devour each other in order to absorb into our own world of thought whatever other such worlds might hold of truth.

But it happens that we are men, each containing

within himself the ontological mystery of personality and freedom: and it is in this very mystery of freedom and personality that genuine tolerance or fellowship takes root. For the basis of good fellowship among men of different creeds is not of the order of the intellect and of ideas, but of the heart and of love. It is friendship, natural friendship, but first and foremost mutual love in God and for God. Love does not go out to essences nor to qualities nor to ideas, but to persons; and it is the mystery of persons and of the divine presence within them which is here in play. This fellowship, then, is not a fellowship of beliefs but the fellowship of men who believe.

The conviction each of us has, rightly or wrongly, regarding the limitations, deficiencies, errors of others does not prevent friendship between minds. In such a fraternal dialogue, there must be a kind of forgiveness and remission, not with regard to ideas—ideas deserve no forgiveness if they are false—but with regard to the condition of him who travels the road at our side. Every believer knows very well that all men will be judged—both himself and all others. But neither he nor another is God, able to pass judgment. What each one is before God, neither the one nor the other knows. Here the "judge not" of the Gospels applies with its full force. We can render judgment concerning ideas, truths, or errors; good or bad actions; character, temperament, and what appears to us of a man's interior disposition. But we are utterly forbidden to judge the innermost heart, that inaccessible center where the person day after day weaves his own fate and ties the bonds binding him to God. When it comes to that, there is only one thing to do, and that is to trust in God. And that is precisely what love for our neighbor prompts us to do.

I should like to dwell a moment on the inner law and the privileges of this friendship of charity, as regards precisely the relations between believers of different religious denominations (as well as between believers and non-believers). I have already made it sufficiently clear that it is wrong to say that such a friendship *transcends* dogma or *exists in spite of* the dogmas of faith. Such a view is inadmissible for all those who believe that the word of God is as absolute as His unity or His transcendence. A mutual love which would be bought at the price of faith, which would base itself on some form of eclecticism, or which, recalling Lessing's parable of the three rings, would say, "I love him who does not have my faith because, after all, I am not sure that my faith is the true faith, and that it bears the device of the true ring," in so saying would reduce faith to a mere historic inheritance and seal it with the seal of agnosticism and relativity. Such a love, for anyone who believes he has heard the word of God, would amount to putting man above God.

That love which is charity, on the contrary, goes first to God, and then to all men, because the more men are loved in God and for God, the more they are loved themselves and in themselves. Moreover this love is born in faith and remains within faith, while at the same time reaching out to those who have not the same faith. That is the very characteristic of love; wherever our love goes, it carries with it our faith.

Nor does the friendship of charity merely make us recognize the *existence* of others—although as a matter of fact here is something already difficult enough for men, and something which includes everything essential. Not only does it make us recognize that another exists, but it makes us recognize that he exists, not as an accident of the empirical world but as a human being who exists before God, and has the right to exist. While remaining within the faith, the friendship of charity helps us to recognize whatever beliefs other than our own include of truth and of dignity, of human and divine values. It makes us respect them, urges us on ever to seek in them everything that is stamped with the mark of man's original greatness and of the prevenient care and generosity of God. It helps us to come to a mutual understanding of one another. It does not make us go beyond our faith but beyond ourselves. In other words, it helps us to purify our faith of the shell of egotism and subjectivity in which we instinctively tend to enclose it. It also inevitably carries with it a sort of heart-rending, attached as is the heart at once to the truth we love and to the neighbor who is ignorant of that truth. This condition is even associated with what is called the "ecumenical" bringing together of divided Christians; how much more is it associated with the labor of bringing into mutual comprehension believers of every denomination.

I distrust any easy and comfortable friendship between believers of all denominations. I mean a friendship which is not accompanied, as it were, by a kind of compunction or soul's sorrow; just as I distrust any universalism which claims to unite in one and the same service of God, and in one and the same transcendental piety—as in some World's Fair Temple— all forms of belief and all forms of worship. The duty of being faithful to the light, and of always following it to the extent that one sees it, is a duty which cannot be evaded. In other words, the problem of conversion, for anyone who feels the spur of God, and to the extent that he is pricked by it, cannot be cast aside, any more than can be cast aside the obligation of the apostolate. And by the same token I also distrust a friendship between believers of the same denomination which is, as it were, easy and comfortable, because in that case charity would be reserved to their fellow-worshippers; there would be a universalism which would limit love to brothers in the same faith, a proselytism which would love another man only in order to convert him and only insofar as he is capable of conversion, a Christianity which would be the Christianity of *good* people as against *bad* people, and which would confuse the order of charity with what a great spiritual writer of the seventeenth century called a police-force order.

The spurious universalism I just alluded to—and which would make all faiths have their stand, window display, and loudspeaker in a World's Fair Temple, on the condition that all of them should confess they are *not sure* that they are conveying the word of God, and that none of them should claim to be the true Faith—is sometimes advocated in the name of Indian wisdom, which teaches a kind of transcendent liberal indifference with respect to any definite creed.

At this point I should like to observe:

First. Such liberal indifference actually applies much less to Indian than to non-Indian creeds, and consequently resembles very much an illusory theme of propaganda. Moreover, as a matter of fact, "Right view or right thinking is the first step in the path of the Buddha, and the word *orthodoxy* is precisely its Greek equivalent. In the Pali scriptures there is much that reads like accounts of heresy trials."[8] Finally, was not Buddhism, which was born in India, persecuted by Brahmanism and expelled from India?

Second. Indian wisdom, be it Brahmanist or Buddhist, does not teach indifference to any supreme truth; it teaches undifferentiation of supreme truth, and this is a definite metaphysical creed indeed. To be sure, Indian metaphysics is rich with invaluable insights and experiences. Yet it is seriously mistaken, insofar as it teaches that the supreme Truth is sheer undifferentiation, and the Supreme Reality so transcendent that it cannot be known in any expressible manner, even through concepts and words which God himself used to reveal Himself to us. This boils down, on the one hand, to disregarding the intellect as such, which can grasp through analogy divine things themselves, and, on the other hand, to forbidding God the right to speak. Then all religious forms are embraced and absorbed in a formless religiosity.

Third. The Western or Westernized caricature of Indian metaphysics, which preaches, in the name of one "sophy" or another, indifference to any religious dogma and equivalence between all religious creeds henceforth decidedly relativized, displays itself a most arrogant dogmatism, asking from its believers unconditional surrender of their minds to teachers who are self-appointed prophets. And the kind of mysticism

[8] Rev. Father Victor White, see footnote 1.

supposedly free from, and superior to, any revealed dogma, which is advocated by this cheap gnosticism, is but spiritual self-complacency or search for powers, which make up for the loss of the sense of truth.

True universalism, as I have insisted all through this chapter, is just the opposite of indifference. The catholicity it implies is not a catholicity of relativism and indistinction, but the catholicity of reason, and first of all the catholicity of the Word of God, which brought salvation to all the human race and to whose mystical body all those who live in grace belong visibly or invisibly.[9] True universalism presupposes the sense of truth and the certainties of faith; it is the universalism of love which uses these very certainties of faith and all the resources of the intellect to understand better, and do full justice to, the other fellow. It is not supra-dogmatic, it is supra-subjective. We find a token of such a universalism of love—not above faith but within faith, not above religious and philosophical truth but within religious and philosophical truth, to the extent to which everyone knows it—in the development of certain discussion groups between Moslems and Christians, for instance, or of certain studies in comparative theology and comparative mys-

[9] See the chapter "Catholicité" in the remarkable book *Chemins de l'Inde et Philosophie Chrétienne* by Olivier Lacombe (Paris: Alsatia, 1956).

ticism. I would like to cite as an example the case of a book written several years ago by two Thomist authors[10] on Moslem theology which proved to be so illuminating for Moslem as well as for Christian readers that a professor of the Al-Hazar University wished to translate it into Arabic.

As to comparative mysticism, it is genuinely comparative only if it avails itself of all the analytical instruments provided by philosophy and theology. According to the principles of Thomist philosophy and theology, it is a fact that, if divine grace exists and bears fruit in them, men of good will who live in non-Christian climates can experience the same *supernatural* mystical union with God "known as unknown"[11] as Christian contemplatives do: it is so, *not* because mystical experience is independent of faith, but because faith in the Redeemer can exist implicitly, together with the grace of Christ, in men who do not know His name, and this faith can develop into grace-given contemplation, through union of love with God. On the other hand, studies in *natural* mysticism have shown that the disciplines of the Yoga, for instance, normally terminate in a mystical experience which is authentic in its own sphere but quite

[10] Louis Gardet and M.-M. Anawati, *Introduction à la Théologie Musulmane* (Paris: Vrin, 1948).

[11] Thomas Aquinas, *Sum. contra Gent.*, III, 49. Cf. Pseudo-Dionysius, *Mystica Theologia*, cap. 2.

different from grace-given contemplation, and has for its object that invaluable reality which is the Self, in its pure act of existing, immediately attained through the void created by intellectual concentration. Thus it is that a Christian can do full justice, in the Christian perspective itself, to mystical experiences which take place in non-Christian religious areas;[12] and he can develop genuine understanding of, and respect for those who are dedicated to these experiences.

I have given these indications only to illustrate the fact that genuine human fellowship is not jeopardized—quite the contrary!—it is fostered by zeal for truth, if only love is there.

[12] Cf. Louis Gardet, *Expériences mystiques en terres non-chrétiennes* (Paris: Alsatia, 1953).

GOD AND SCIENCE

Preliminary Remarks

IN THE realm of culture, science now holds sway over human civilization. But at the same time science has, in the realm of the mind, entered a period of deep and fecund trouble and self-examination. Scientists have to face the problems of over-specialization, and a general condition of permanent crisis which stems from an extraordinarily fast swarming of discoveries and theoretical renewals, and perhaps from the very approach peculiar to modern science. They have, in general, got rid of the idea that it is up to science to organize human life and society and to supersede ethics and religion by providing men with the standards and values on which their destiny depends. Finally—and this is the point with which I am especially concerned in this essay—the cast of mind of scientists regarding religion and philosophy, as it appeared in the majority of them a century ago, has now profoundly changed.

There are, no doubt, atheists among scientists, as there are in any other category of people; but atheism is not regarded by them as required by science. The old notion of a basic opposition between science and religion is progressively passing away. No conflict between them is possible, Robert Millikan declared. In many scientists there is an urge either toward more or less vague religiosity or toward definite religious faith; and there is an urge, too, toward philosophical unification of knowledge. But the latter urge still remains, more often than not, imbued with a kind of intellectual ambiguity.

No wonder, then, that the subject with which we are dealing—what is the relation of modern science to man's knowledge of God—demands a rather delicate, sometimes complicated analysis. In order to clear the ground, I shall begin with a few observations concerning the characteristic approach and way of knowledge peculiar to science as it has developed since post-Renaissance and post-Cartesian times and become in our day, through an effort of reflection upon its own procedures, more and more explicitly aware of itself.

I do not disregard the differences in nature which separate physics from other sciences, such as biology or anthropology, for instance. Yet physics is the queen of modern sciences, which, even when they cannot be perfectly mathematized, tend to resemble physics to one degree or another. So it is that for the sake of brevity I shall, while speaking of modern science, have modern physics especially in view.

Modern science has progressively "freed" or separated itself from philosophy (more specifically from the philosophy of nature) thanks to mathematics—that is to say by becoming a particular type of knowledge whose data are facts drawn by our senses or instruments from the world of nature, but whose intelligibility is mathematical intelligibility. As a result, the primary characteristic of the approach to reality peculiar to science may therefore be described in the following way: that which can be observed and measured, and the ways through which observation and measurement are to be achieved, and the more or less unified mathematical reconstruction of such data—these things alone have a meaning for the scientist as such.

The field of knowledge particular to science is therefore limited to experience (as Kant understood the word). And when the basic notions that science uses derive from concepts traditionally used by common sense and philosophy, such as the notions of nature, matter, or causality, these basic notions are recast and restricted by science, so as to apply only to the field of experience and observable phenomena, understood and expressed in a certain set of mathematical signs. Thus it is that physicists may construct the concept of antimatter, for example, which has a meaning for them, but not for the layman or for the philosopher.

The expression "science of phenomena" is currently

employed to designate our modern sciences. Such an expression is valid only if we realize, on the one hand, that the phenomena in question are (especially as far as physics is concerned) mathematized phenomena, and, on the other hand, that they are not an object separate from but an aspect of that reality *in se* which is Nature. Let us say that science is a genuine, though oblique, knowledge of nature; it attains reality, but in its phenomenal aspect (in other words, in the aspect of reality which is definable through observation and measurement), and by the instrumentality of entities, especially mathematical entities, which may be "real" and relate to what Aristotelian realism called "quantity" as an accident of material substance, or may be purely ideal entities (*entia rationis*) and mere symbols grounded on data of observation and measurement.

Such ideal entities are the price paid for a tremendous privilege, namely the mathematical reconstruction of the data of experience. I observed a moment ago that modern science has, thanks to mathematics, freed itself from philosophy. At first mathematics were used by the sciences of nature in the framework of sense experience only. It has happened, however, that for more than a century mathematics themselves, starting with non-Euclidian geometries, have been breaking loose, more definitely and more completely than before, from the world of experience, and insisting on the possibility of developing—in the realm of merely logical or ideal being (*ens rationis*) —an infinite multiplicity of demonstrably consistent systems based on freely chosen and utterly opposed "axioms" or postulates. Consequently the science of phenomena (particularly physics) became able to pick out among various possible mathematical languages or conceptualizations, which make sense only to the mathematician, and deal with entities existing only within the mind, the one most appropriate to a given set of phenomena (while other sets of phenomena may be made mathematically intelligible through quite another conceptualization). So it is that from the point of view of common sense everything in the world capsizes in the highest and most comprehensive theories of contemporary physics as in Chagall's pictures. Modern science of phenomena has its feet on earth and uses its hands to gather not only correctly observed and measured facts, but also a great many notions and explanations which offer our minds real entities; yet it has its head in a mathematical heaven, populated with various crowds of signs and merely ideal, even not intuitively thinkable entities.

These ideal entities constructed by the mind are symbols which enable science to manipulate the world, while knowing it as unknown, for then, in those higher regions where creative imagination is more at work than classical induction, science is intent only on translating the multifarious observable aspects of the world into coherent systems of signs.

The fact remains that the prime incentive of the scientist is the urge to know reality. Belief in the existence of the mysterious reality of the universe precedes scientific inquiry in the scientist's mind, and a longing (possibly more or less repressed) to attain this reality in its inner depths is naturally latent in him.

But as a scientist his knowledge is limited to a mathematical (or quasi-mathematical) understanding and reconstruction of the observable and measurable aspects of nature taken in their inexhaustible detail.

"Exclusive" Scientists and "Liberal" Scientists

A distinction must be made between two categories of scientists, whom I would like to call, on the one hand, exclusive scientists, and, on the other hand, liberal scientists. This distinction has nothing to do with science itself, for in both categories men endowed with the highest scientific capacities can be found; but it is quite important from the point of view of culture.

"Exclusive" scientists are systematically convinced that science is the only kind of genuine rational knowledge of which man is capable. For them nothing can be known to human reason except through the means and intellectual equipment of science. Exclusive scientists may be of positivist persuasion, and consequently reject any religious belief, save perhaps some kind of mythically constructed atheistic religion, like Auguste Comte's religion of humanity, which its high priest conceived of as a "positive regeneration of fetishism," or like Julian Huxley's "religion without revelation," which mistakes itself for a product of the "scientific method." Or they may shun positivist prohibitions, and superadd to scientific knowledge a genuine, even deep religious faith, but which supposedly belongs to the world of feeling and pure irrationality. In no case is it possible, in their eyes, to establish the existence of God with rational certainty.

To tell the truth, the assertion that there is no valid rational knowledge except that of observable and measurable phenomena is self-destructive (it itself is quite another thing than a mere expression of inter-related phenomena). No wonder, consequently, that in contradistinction to exclusive scientists, "liberal" scientists are ready to look for a rational grasping of things which passes beyond phenomena, and even (when they are perfectly liberal scientists—I think for instance of an eminent chemist like Sir Hugh Taylor, or an eminent physicist like Léon Brillouin) to admit the necessity of philosophy and of a properly philosophical equipment in order to make such grasping feasible, and so to complement the knowledge of nature provided by the sciences.

Nothing is more rational than the kind of extension of Niels Bohr's "principle of complementarity" implied by the cast of mind of these scientists. For, thus extended, this principle means simply that in two different fields of knowledge, or at two specifically distinct levels in our approach to reality, two different aspects in existing things (the phenomenal and the ontological aspect) call for two different explanations (for instance "Man's cerebral activity is stimulated by such or such chemical" and "Man has a spiritual soul")—which are moreover perfectly compatible, since they have to do with two essentially diverse objects to be grasped in things (so the medical approach to a person as a patient and the aesthetic approach to the same person as a poet are both distinct and compatible).

Einstein belonged to the category of liberal scientists. For many years his notion of God was akin to that of Spinoza. Yet, as recent studies have shown, he came, with the progress of age and reflection, to consider the existence of that personal God whom he first doubted as required by the way in which nature lends itself to the rationalization of phenomena operated by science. As he said in an interview in 1950, far from being an atheist he "believed on the contrary in a personal God."[1] Such a conviction meant in no way that the existence of God was supposedly a conclusion established by science, or a principle of explanation used by it. It meant that the existence of God is a conclusion philosophically established with regard to the very possibility of science.

Heisenberg[2] and Oppenheimer[3] are also liberal scientists. So was, at least virtually, Max Planck, though it was under the cloak of science that every bit of philosophizing effort in him was concealed.[4] He believed in an "all-powerful intelligence which governs the universe," but not in a personal God, and he thought that we could and should "identify with each other . . . the order of the universe which is implied by the sciences of nature and the God whom religion holds to exist." Such statements definitely transcend the field of experience and measurable data, though they remain inherently ambiguous: for how could an all-powerful reason govern the universe if it were not personal? The God whom religion holds to exist is a transcendent God, who causes the order of the

[1] Cf. Karlheinz Schauder, "Weltbild und Religion bei Albert Einstein," in *Frankfurter Hefte*, June 1959, p. 426.

[2] Cf. Werner Heisenberg, *Physics and Philosophy*, New York: Harper, 1958.

[3] Cf. Robert Oppenheimer, "The Mystery of Matter," in *Adventures of the Mind*, New York: Alfred A. Knopf, 1959.

[4] André George, *Autobiographie scientifique de Max Planck*, Paris: Albin Michel, 1960, pp. 14, 122, 215, 217.

universe, but his philosophical "identification" with this order would make him consubstantial with the world, as the God of the Stoics was.

Such intellectual ambiguity is not infrequent. I have already mentioned the fact. Let us consider it now a little more closely. I would say that the ambiguity in question is essential in exclusive scientists, so far as they take a step outside science itself. They emphatically deny the validity of any kind of rational knowledge of reality which is not science itself. As a result, if they are not of positivist persuasion, and do not think that all we can know is phenomena alone, in other words, if, recognizing that phenomena are but an aspect of a deeper reality, they endeavor to go beyond phenomena, they do so through an extrapolation of scientific notions which, brilliant as it may be, is essentially arbitrary; or, looking for a "noetic integrator," they borrow it from some kind of metaphysics unaware of itself and disguised as science—and there is no worse metaphysics than disguised metaphysics.

As regards liberal scientists the picture is basically different. I would say that the ambiguity we are discussing can still most often be found in them, but as something accidental, not essential to their cast of mind; so that, as a matter of fact, there are good grounds to hope that more and more of them will, in the process of time, free themselves from it—when philosophers will become more intent on meditating on the sciences and learning their languages, and scientists more familiar with the approach and language of philosophy (each one realizing at the same time that the language or languages of the others are valid instruments only for the others' work).

If a liberal scientist undertakes to go beyond the horizons of science and tackle the philosophical aspects of reality, he too is liable to yield to the temptation of making the concepts worked out by science into the very components of his meta-scientific enterprise. The trouble is that one can no more philosophize with non-philosophical instruments than paint with a flute or a piano.

But such a state of affairs is only a side-effect of the fact that scientists, however liberal, are prone, as everyone is, to over-value the intellectual equipment they have tested in their particular field, and in the handling of which they have full competence. Liberal scientists do not, for all that, systematically deny the validity of another, perhaps more appropriate, intellectual equipment; they are aware, moreover, of the philosophical nature of their own effort of reflection upon science and its procedures; and by the very fact they are, at least implicitly, prepared to recognize the rights of that purely or genuinely philosophical approach in which they still often hesitate to put their own trust. That is why the ambiguity of the way in which many of them go in for philosophy is accidental ambiguity.

Furthermore, being accidental, such ambiguity can be removed; the best proof of this is the fact that in actual existence it has been most explicitly removed in some scientists who, when it comes to philosophical matters, do not mind using the strict philosophical approach. At this point I am thinking in particular of the Epilogue which the distinguished physiologist Andrew Ivy wrote for the book "The Evidence of God," in which he insists that God's existence can be rationally demonstrated with absolute certainty.[5] Though a professional philosopher would probably have added a few considerations on knowledge through analogy and the non-restricted value of the notion of cause, these pages written by a scientist are, as they stand, a remarkable piece of philosophy, which enters with perfect intellectual frankness and with the appropriate intellectual equipment a sphere inaccessible to the instruments of science, and which gives to a truth intuitively known to the intellect like the principle of causality its full ontological bearing, so as to recognize the necessity of a Prime Cause that absolutely transcends the whole field of experience.

[5] Cf. *The Evidence of God in an Expanding Universe,* edited by J. G. Monsma, by forty American Scientists, with an Epilogue by Dr. Andrew Ivy (New York: Putnam, 1958).

The Crucial Question

The crucial question for our age of culture is, thus, whether reality can be approached and known, not only "phenomenally" by science, but also "ontologically" by philosophy.

This question is still more crucial for the common man than for the scientist. For the impact of the habits of thinking prevalent in an industrial civilization, in which manipulation of the world through science and technique plays the chief part, results in a loss of the sense of being in the minds of a large number of people, who are not scientists but grant rational value to facts and figures only. Whereas exclusive scientists know at least what science is and what its limitations are, the people of whom I am speaking have no experience of science, and they believe all the more naïvely that science is the only valid rational approach to reality, nay more, that science has all the rational answers which human life can need.

Consequently, any rational knowledge of God's existence—either pre-philosophical (by the simple natural use of reason) or philosophical (by the use of reason trained in philosophical disciplines)—is a dead letter as far as they are concerned.

Persons whose intellect has shrunk in this way may adhere to some religious creed and have a religious belief in God—either as a gift of divine grace, or as a response to irrational needs, or as a result of their adjustment to a given environment. But they are atheists as far as reason is concerned. Such a situation is utterly abnormal. Religious faith is above reason, but normally presupposes the rational conviction of God's existence.

At this point we must lay stress on the nature of philosophy as contradistinguished from science, and insist that philosophy is an autonomous discipline, which has its own instruments; so that it is not enough to add to scientific knowledge even a most intelligent philosophical reflection; the proper philosophical training and proper philosophical equipment are necessary.

Let us say that whereas science, or phenomenal knowledge, offers us, with wonderful richness paid for by revolutionary changes, coded maps of what matter and nature are as to the multifarious observable and measurable interactions which occur in them, philosophy makes us grasp, with greater stability paid for by limitation to essentials, what things are in the intrinsic reality of their being. Though carrying common sense and the natural language to an essentially higher level, philosophy is in continuity with them, and is based on the perceptive (not only constructive) power of the intellect as well as on sense experience. In other words, being is the primary object of philosophy, as it is of human reason; and all notions worked out by philosophy are intelligible in terms of being, not of observation and measurement.

As a result, we have to realize that in the very universe of experience philosophy (the philosophy of nature) deals with aspects and explanations in which science is not interested. Thus matter (that is, material substances) is composed, in the eyes of old but still valid Aristotelian hylomorphism, of two elements: pure and indetermined potentiality (*materia prima*), and determinative form or entelechy (which, in man, is spiritual soul); whereas for science matter (or mass, that is, a given set of measurable data expressed in mathematical equations) is composed of certain particles, most of them impermanent, scrutinized by nuclear physics. It is up to philosophy to try to bring into some sort of unity our knowledge of nature, not by making science's explanations parts of its own explanations, but by interpreting them in its own light. In order to do so, it will have, in the first place, to enlighten us about *the procedure of science itself*, which constructs both ideal or symbolical entities *founded on actual measurement*, and complex notions where reality phenomenally grasped mingles inextricably with these merely ideal entities. In the second place, philosophy will have to determine what kind of *ontological foundation* may be assigned to such or such of these notions, or sets of notions, peculiar to science. In the third place, philosophy will have to point out—and to improve and re-adjust, each time this is needed—*the truths of its own* which have some connection with scientific theories, and especially with all the treasure of facts and factual assertions which is mustered and continually increased by science.

Being, furthermore, is not limited to the field of sense experience; it goes beyond. And the basic concepts of reason which deal with being as such, even though they apply first to the realm of experience, can apply too—in an "analogical" manner—to realities which transcend experience. As a result philosophy (this time I do not mean the philosophy of nature, I mean metaphysics) can attain to realities which escape sense experience and sense verification, in other words which belong to the spiritual or "supra-sensible" order.[6]

Let us remember at this point that philosophy is but a superior stage in the natural use of reason, at the level of a knowledge which is not only knowledge but wisdom, and which (in contradistinction to common sense) is critically elaborated and completely articulated. Prior to philosophy, the natural use of reason is natural in an additional sense (in the sense of untrained and merely spontaneous); with philos-

[6] Cf. our books *The Degrees of Knowledge*, new translation, New York: Scribner, 1959; and *Approaches to God*, New York: Harper, 1954.

ophy it is perfected by reflectivity, fully mature, and capable of explicit demonstration, aware of its own validity.

It is by virtue of the very nature of human reason —either untrained or philosophically perfected—that the concept of cause and the principle of causality can lead us beyond the field of experience. As Dr. Ivy has rightly pointed out,[7] if the child uses the principle of causality in asking why things exist, he does so not by reason of the transitory peculiarities of "childish mentality," but, on the contrary, because he is awakening to genuine intellectual life.

There is, thus, a pre-philosophical, simply natural knowledge of God's existence. It can be described as starting from the primordial intuition of existence, and immediately perceiving that Being-with-nothingness, or things which could possibly not be—my own being, which is liable to death—necessarily presuppose Being-without-nothingness, that is, absolute or self-subsisting Being, which causes and activates all beings. This pre-philosophical knowledge can also be described as a spontaneous application of the principle: no artifact is possible without a maker.

And there is, in the realm of metaphysical wisdom, a philosophical knowledge of God's existence, which is able fully to justify itself and uses ways of arguing that proceed with full rational rigor.

[7] Cf. *supra*, p. 55, footnote 5.

The Philosophical Proofs of
God's Existence

The "five ways" of Thomas Aquinas are the classical example of the philosophical approach to God of which I just spoke. It seems relevant to give at this point some idea of them, at least of the first and the last two.

The first way proceeds from Motion or Change. There is no fact more obvious here below than the fact of change, through which a thing becomes what it was not. But no thing can give to itself what it does not have, at least in potency, and potency cannot pass to actuation by itself alone. Everywhere where there is motion or change (even if it is self-motion as in living beings), there is something else which is causing the change. Now if the cause in question is itself subject to change, then it is moved or activated by another agent. But it is impossible to regress from agent to agent without end: if there were not a First Agent, the reason for the action of all others would never be posited in existence. So it is necessary to stop at a Prime Cause, itself uncaused, absolutely exempt from any change for it is absolutely perfect.

In the same manner the second way, which proceeds from Efficient Causes at work in the world, and the third way, which proceeds from Contingency and Necessity in things, lead to a Prime Cause without which all other causes would neither be nor act, and which exists with absolute necessity, in the infinite transcendence of the very *esse* subsisting by itself.

The fourth way proceeds from the Degrees which are in things. It is a fact that there are degrees of value or perfection in things. But, on the one hand, where-ever there are degrees it is necessary that there exist, somewhere, a supreme degree; and on the other hand one thing is good and another is better, but there can always be another still better, so that there is no su-preme degree in the possible degrees of goodness, or beauty, or finally being, of which things are capable. Goodness, beauty, being are not in their fulness in any one of the things we touch and see. The supreme degree of goodness, of beauty, of being, exists *else-where*, in a Prime Being which causes all that there is of goodness, beauty, and being in things, a First Cause which does not *have* goodness, beauty, and being, but *is* self-subsisting Being, Goodness, and Beauty.

The fifth way proceeds from the intrinsic Order and purposeful Governance of the world. The very fact that in the material universe things are engaged in a system of stable relations and that a certain order among them exists and endures shows that they do not result from chance. A purpose is at work in that republic of natures which is the world. But such pur-pose cannot proceed from the things which compose the world of matter, and which are devoid of under-standing. This purpose or intention must exist in an intellect on which things depend in their very essence and natural activities. Thus in the last analysis it is necessary to recognize the existence of a transcendent Intelligence, the existing of which is its very intellec-tion, and which is the Prime Cause of all beings.

I have summarized these ways to God in my own language and in the briefest possible fashion, leaving aside all particular examples, accidental to the demon-stration, which were part of the imagery provided to Thomas Aquinas by the physics of his time.

The ways in question pertain to the philosophical order. The notion of cause has here its full ontological import, which connotes productivity in being, in con-tradistinction to the mere relationships between phe-nomena which science considers and in which a given phenomenon is a dependent variable of another. Fur-thermore, we are led by rational argumentation to a Prime Cause which is absolutely and infinitely tran-scendent, and which the very concept of cause, like those of being, of goodness, of intelligence, etc., at-tains only "by analogy" or in the mirror of things: what all these concepts mean with respect to God is only similar to—but basically different from—what they mean with respect to things accessible to us; we don't grasp it *in itself*. God exists as no other being exists, He is good as no other being is good, He knows and loves as no other being does.

It must be noted that considered in their very substance the "five ways" of Thomas Aquinas stand fast against any criticism. Modern philosophy has been in this connection the victim of a tragic misunderstanding. Descartes believed that from the sole idea of an infinitely perfect being the existence of this being necessarily followed (the so-called "ontological argument"). Kant rightly stated that such "proof" was no proof at all. But he also stated—quite mistakenly—that all other proofs of God's existence implied the validity of the ontological argument and rested on it; as a result, no valid proof was possible. And Kant's successors followed on Kant's heels. Yet it is crystal clear that Thomas Aquinas' five ways do not start from the *idea* of an infinitely perfect being; they proceed in the opposite manner; they start from certain *facts*, quite general and quite undeniable; and from these facts they infer the necessary existence of a First Cause—which is infinitely perfect. Infinite perfection is at the end, not at the beginning of the demonstration.

Finally let us add that there are other ways, too, than the classical five ways. I myself have proposed a "sixth way." As a matter of fact there are for man as many ways of knowing that God exists as there are steps forward for him on the earth or paths to his own heart. For all our perishable treasures of being and beauty are besieged on all sides by the immensity and eternity of the One Who Is.

Sciences as Witnessing to God's Existence

Among all these approaches to God, one particularly significant for the man of our present civilization is provided by science itself. The sciences of phenomena —though they remain enclosed in the field of experience—bear testimony to the existence of God in a double manner. Here, as I previously noted, it is not a question of what science itself tells us, but of the very existence and possibility of science.

In the first place: if nature were not intelligible there would be no science. Nature is not perfectly and absolutely intelligible; and the sciences do not try to come to grips with nature's intelligibility taken in itself (that is the job of philosophy). They rather reach for it in an oblique fashion, dealing with it only insofar as it is steeped in, and masked by, the observable and measurable data of the world of experience, and can be translated into mathematical intelligibility. Yet the intelligibility of nature is the very ground of those relational constancies which are the "laws"—including that category of laws which deal only with probabilities—to which science sees phenomena submitted; and it is the very ground, in particular, of the highest explanatory systems, with all the symbols, ideal entities, and code languages they employ (and with all that in them which is still incomplete, arbitrary, and puzzlingly lacking in harmony) that science constructs on observation and measurement.

Now how would things be intelligible if they did not proceed from an intelligence? In the last analysis a Prime Intelligence must exist, which is itself Intellection and Intelligibility in pure act, and which is the first principle of the intelligibility and essences of things, and causes order to exist in them, as well as an infinitely complex network of regular relationships, whose fundamental mysterious unity our reason dreams of rediscovering in its own way.

Such an approach to God's existence is a variant of Thomas Aquinas' fifth way. Its impact was secretly present in Einstein's famous saying: "God does not play dice," which, no doubt, used the word God in a merely figurative sense, and meant only: "nature does not result from a throw of the dice," yet the very fact implicitly postulated the existence of the divine Intellect.

But science offers us a second philosophical approach, which, this time, relates to man's intellect. The sciences of phenomena, and the manner in which they contrive ways of knowing and mastering nature —ceaselessly inveigling it into more and more pre-

cise observations and measurements, and finally catch-
ing it in sets of more and more perfectly systematized
signs—give evidence, in a particularly striking manner, of the power that human intelligence puts to
work in the very universe of sense experience. Now
the intelligence of man—imperfect as it is, and obliged
to use an irreducible multiplicity of types and per-
spectives of knowledge—is a spiritual activity which
can neither proceed from matter nor be self-subsisting, and therefore limitless and all-knowing. It has a
higher source, of which it is a certain participation.
In other words, it necessarily requires the existence
of a Prime, transcendent, and absolutely perfect Intelligence, which is pure Intellection in act and whose
being is its very Intellection.

This second approach is a variant of Thomas Aquinas' fourth way.

To conclude, let us remark that our knowledge of
the created world naturally reverberates in the very
reverence and awe with which our reason knows the
Creator, and on the very notion, deficient as it is and
will ever be, that we have of His ways.

By the very fact that science enlarges our horizons
with respect to this world, and makes us know better
—though in an oblique way—that created reality
which is the mirror in which God's perfections are

analogically known, science helps our minds to pay tribute to God's grandeur.

A number of the most basic notions and explanatory theories of modern science, especially of modern physics, recoil from being translated into natural language, or from being represented in terms of the imagination. Nevertheless a certain picture of the world emerges from modern science; and this picture (unification of matter and energy, physical indeterminism, a space-time continuum which implies that space and time are not empty pre-existing forms but come to existence with things and through things; gravitational fields which by reason of the curvation of space exempt gravitation from requiring any particular force, and outwit ether and attraction; a cosmos of electrons and stars in which the stars are the heavenly laboratories of elements, a universe which is finite but whose limits cannot be attained, and which dynamically evolves toward higher forms of individuation and concentration) constitutes a kind of framework or imagery more suited to many positions of a sound philosophy of nature than that which was provided by Newtonian science.

Furthermore, at the core of this imagery there are a few fundamental concepts which, inherent in modern science and essential to it, have a direct impact on our philosophical view of nature.

In the first place I shall mention all the complex

regularities (presupposed by statistical laws themselves), and the mixture of organization and chance, resulting in a kind of elusive, imperfectly knowable, and still more striking order, that matter reveals in the world of microphysics. It makes our idea of the order of nature exceedingly more refined and more astonishing. And it makes us look at the author of this order with still more admiration and natural reverence. In the Book of Job, Behemoth and Leviathan were called to witness to divine omnipotence. One single atom may be called to witness too, as well as the hippopotamus and the crocodile. If the heavens declare the glory of God, so does the world of micro-particles and micro-waves.

In the second place comes the notion of evolution: evolution of the whole universe of matter, and, in particular, evolution of living organisms. Like certain most general tenets of science, evolution is less a demonstrated conclusion than a kind of primary concept which has such power in making phenomena decipherable that once expressed it becomes almost impossible for the scientific mind to do without it. Now if it is true that in opposition to the immobile archetypes and ever-recurrent cycles of pagan antiquity, Christianity taught men to conceive history both as irreversible and as running in a definite direction, then it may be said that by integrating in science the dimension of time and history, the idea of evolution has given to our knowledge of nature a certain affinity with what the Christian view of things is on a quite different plane. In any case, the genesis of elements and the various phases of the history of the heavens, and, in the realm of life, the historical development of an immense diversity of evolutive branches ("phyla"), all this, if it is understood in the proper philosophical perspective, presupposes the transcendent God as the prime cause of evolution—preserving in existence created things and the impetus present in them, moving them from above so that superior forms may emerge from inferior ones, and, when man is to appear at the peak of the series of vertebrates, intervening in a special way and creating *ex nihilo* the spiritual and immortal soul of the first man and of every individual of the new species. Thus evolution correctly understood offers us a spectacle whose greatness and universality make the activating omnipresence of God only more tellingly sensed by our minds.

I do not believe, moreover, that science fosters a particularly optimistic view of nature. Every progress in evolution is dearly paid for: miscarried attempts, merciless struggle everywhere. The more detailed our knowledge of nature becomes, the more we see, together with the element of generosity and progression which radiates from being, the law of degradation, the powers of destruction and death, the implacable voracity which are also inherent in the world of matter. And when it comes to man, surrounded and invaded as he is by a host of warping forces, psychology and anthropology are but an account of the fact that, while being essentially superior to all of them, he is the most unfortunate of animals. So it is that when its vision of the world is enlightened by science, the intellect which religious faith perfects realizes still better that nature, however good in its own order, does not suffice, and that if the deepest hopes of mankind are not destined to turn to mockery, it is because a God-given energy better than nature is at work in us.